AVERY WRIGHT

The Final Warning

A Deep Dive into the IPCC's Final Warning

amazon publishing

Contents

Thank You

Dear Reader,

Thank you for taking the time to read "The Final Warning: A Deep Dive into the IPCC's Final Warning." We hope that this book has provided you with valuable insights into the urgency of the climate crisis and the need for immediate action.

The IPCC's Final Warning is a wake-up call for the entire world to address the climate crisis. We hope that this book has provided you with a deeper understanding of the challenges and barriers to climate action, as well as pathways to climate action and successful examples of climate action.

We believe that the urgency of the climate crisis requires immediate action from governments, businesses, and individuals. It is the responsibility of all of us to take action to reduce greenhouse gas emissions and mitigate the impacts of climate change.

We hope that this book has inspired you to take action to address the climate crisis and transition to a sustainable, low-carbon future. Together, we can make a difference and create a better future for ourselves and future generations.

Thank you again for reading "The Final Warning: A Deep Dive

into the IPCC's Final Warning." We appreciate your interest and support.

Sincerely,
  Avery Wright

1

Introduction

The Intergovernmental Panel on Climate Change (IPCC), comprised of the world's top climate researchers, has issued a "final warning" regarding the climate crisis. The comprehensive review boils down to one clear message: act now, before it's too late. The IPCC has released the final part of its six-part assessment on March 20, 2023, which highlights the urgency and severity of the climate crisis.

The IPCC's Final Warning is a wake-up call to the entire world. The report warns that the world is already approaching the limit to which it is able to adapt to severe changes, as weather extremes are "increasingly driving displacement." This warning comes at a critical time when the world is grappling with the effects of climate change, including rising sea levels, extreme weather conditions, and ecological disasters.

The purpose of this chapter is to provide a deep dive into the IPCC's Final Warning. This chapter will explore the key findings and recommendations of the assessment and highlight the impacts of climate change on the environment and society.

The IPCC's Assessment on Climate Change

- Overview of the six-part assessment
- Key findings and recommendations
- Impacts of climate change on the environment and society
- Extremes of climate change and their effects
- The world's ability to adapt to climate change

The IPCC's Final Warning is the culmination of a six-part assessment that began in 2018. The assessment involved more than 200 scientists from around the world, who analyzed the latest scientific research on climate change.

The key findings of the assessment are alarming. The report warns that the world is on the brink of irrevocable damage, and immediate action is needed to prevent catastrophic consequences. The assessment highlights the impacts of climate change on the environment and society, including the destruction of ecosystems, food insecurity, and displacement of millions of people.

The report also warns about the extremes of climate change and their effects, such as increasing temperatures, more frequent and intense heatwaves, heavy rainfall, and more frequent and severe droughts. These extremes are having a devastating impact on people and the environment, leading to the destruction of homes and livelihoods.

Moreover, the IPCC's assessment warns that the world's ability to adapt to climate change is limited. As climate change continues, the world will face more severe and irreversible consequences. The report emphasizes that immediate action is necessary to avoid reaching the tipping point beyond which the world will no longer be able to adapt to climate change.

The Urgency of Climate Action

- The need for immediate action
- Consequences of inaction
- The IPCC's call for a radical transformation of society
- The role of governments, businesses, and individuals in addressing the crisis

The IPCC's Final Warning emphasizes the need for immediate action to address the climate crisis. The report warns that delaying action will result in irreversible consequences that will affect future generations. The consequences of inaction include rising sea levels, more frequent and intense heatwaves, and the destruction of ecosystems.

To address the climate crisis, the IPCC calls for a radical transformation of society. This transformation requires a shift towards a low-carbon economy, the use of renewable energy sources, and the adoption of sustainable practices in all sectors of the economy.

Governments, businesses, and individuals all have a crucial role to play in addressing the climate crisis. Governments must take decisive action to reduce greenhouse gas emissions and promote sustainable practices. Businesses must adopt sustainable practices and invest in renewable energy sources. Individuals can reduce their carbon footprint by adopting sustainable lifestyles and supporting sustainable practices.

Challenges and Barriers to Climate Action

- Political and economic barriers to climate action
- The influence of the fossil fuel industry
- Technological and infrastructural challenges

Over coming social and psychological barriers

While urgent action is needed to address the climate crisis, there are several challenges and barriers that must be overcome. One of the biggest challenges is political and economic barriers to climate action. In many cases, political leaders are reluctant to take action on climate change due to fears of economic consequences or political backlash. Additionally, some industries, particularly the fossil fuel industry, have significant influence on policy decisions and may resist efforts to shift towards sustainable practices.

Technological and infrastructural challenges also present obstacles to climate action. For example, the transition to renewable energy sources and sustainable practices may require significant investment in new technology and infrastructure. Additionally, there may be challenges in scaling up these practices to meet the needs of entire communities or countries.

Social and psychological barriers may also hinder progress towards addressing the climate crisis. Some people may feel overwhelmed by the scale of the problem or uncertain about the effectiveness of individual actions. Others may resist change due to concerns about the impact on their daily lives or the economy.

Moving Forward

- · A. Pathways to climate action
- · B. Successful examples of climate action
- · C. Addressing climate change as a global issue
- · D. Hope for the future

Despite these challenges, there are pathways to climate action that can be successful. This includes a combination of policy initiatives, technological advancements, and individual actions. There are also many successful examples of climate action around the world, from the adoption of renewable energy sources to the implementation of sustainable transportation systems.

Addressing climate change is a global issue that requires collaboration and cooperation across nations and industries. International agreements such as the Paris Agreement provide a framework for countries to work together towards common goals, while initiatives such as the United Nations Framework Convention on Climate Change promote international cooperation on climate action.

Despite the urgency and severity of the climate crisis, there is hope for the future. Through collective action and sustained effort, it is possible to create a sustainable, low-carbon future that protects the environment and promotes economic prosperity.

Final Words

- Recap of key points
- Final thoughts on the IPCC's Final Warning
- Call to action

The IPCC's Final Warning is a wake-up call to the world, highlighting the urgency and severity of the climate crisis. Immediate action is needed to prevent catastrophic consequences and create a sustainable, low-carbon future. Governments, businesses, and individuals all have a crucial role to play in addressing the climate crisis, and overcoming challenges and barriers to climate action is essential to achieving success.

As we move forward, it is important to remember that addressing the climate crisis is not only a scientific or political issue but a moral imperative. By taking action today, we can create a better, more sustainable world for future generations.

2

The IPCC's Assessment on Climate Change

The IPCC's assessment on climate change is a comprehensive review of the latest scientific research on climate change. The assessment is divided into six parts, each addressing different aspects of the climate crisis. This chapter will provide an overview of the six-part assessment, highlight the key findings and recommendations, and examine the impacts of climate change on the environment and society.

Overview of the Six-Part Assessment

The IPCC's assessment is a multi-year effort involving hundreds of scientists from around the world. The assessment is divided into six parts, each focusing on a different aspect of the climate crisis. The six parts are as follows:

- **The Physical Science Basis:** This part focuses on the physical science of climate change, including the causes and impacts of climate change, and the methods for predicting future climate change.

- **Impacts, Vulnerability, and Adaptation:** This part focuses on the impacts of climate change on human and natural systems, and the vulnerabilities and adaptations needed to mitigate these impacts.
- **Mitigation of Climate Change:** This part focuses on the methods for reducing greenhouse gas emissions and mitigating the impacts of climate change.
- **Carbon Dioxide Removal and Sequestration:** This part focuses on the methods for removing carbon dioxide from the atmosphere and sequestering it in the earth or oceans.
- **Climate Change and Health:** This part focuses on the impacts of climate change on human health, and the strategies for mitigating these impacts.
- **Societal and Ethical Issues:** This part focuses on the societal and ethical issues related to climate change, including equity, justice, and human rights.

Key Findings and Recommendations

The key findings of the IPCC's assessment are alarming. The report warns that the world is on the brink of irrevocable damage, and immediate action is needed to prevent catastrophic consequences. The assessment highlights the following key findings:

- Human activities are the primary cause of climate change. The burning of fossil fuels, deforestation, and other human activities are releasing large amounts of greenhouse gases into the atmosphere, leading to rising temperatures, sea level rise, and extreme weather conditions.

- Climate change is already affecting the environment and society. The impacts of climate change include the destruction of ecosystems, food insecurity, and displacement of millions of people.
- The world's ability to adapt to climate change is limited. As climate change continues, the world will face more severe and irreversible consequences. Immediate action is necessary to avoid reaching the tipping point beyond which the world will no longer be able to adapt to climate change.

The IPCC's assessment also provides recommendations for addressing the climate crisis. The report calls for a radical transformation of society, including a shift towards a low-carbon economy, the use of renewable energy sources, and the adoption of sustainable practices in all sectors of the economy.

Impacts of Climate Change on the Environment and Society

The impacts of climate change on the environment and society are widespread and severe. Rising temperatures, sea level rise, and extreme weather conditions are leading to the destruction of ecosystems and the displacement of millions of people. Some of the specific impacts of climate change include:

- **Rising sea levels:** As temperatures rise, glaciers and ice caps are melting, causing sea levels to rise. This can lead to flooding in coastal areas, which can damage infrastructure and homes.

- **Extreme weather conditions:** Climate change is causing more frequent and intense heatwaves, heavy rainfall, and more frequent and severe droughts. These extremes are having a devastating impact on people and the environment, leading to the destruction of homes and livelihoods.
- **Destruction of ecosystems:** Climate change is causing the destruction of ecosystems, including coral reefs, forests, and wetlands. This can lead to the loss of biodiversity and the disruption of ecosystems, which can have severe consequences for human society.

Extremes of Climate Change and their Effects

The extremes of climate change are having severe consequences on the environment and society. The IPCC's assessment warns that as climate change continues, the world will face more frequent and severe heatwaves, heavy rainfall, and droughts. These extremes are having a devastating impact on people and the environment, leading to the destruction of homes and livelihoods. Some of the specific impacts of the extremes of climate change include:

More frequent and intense heatwaves: As temperatures rise, heatwaves are becoming more frequent and intense. This can lead to increased mortality rates, particularly among the elderly and vulnerable populations.

Heavy rainfall and flooding: Climate change is causing more frequent and intense rainfall, leading to flooding in many regions of the world. This can damage infrastructure and homes, leading to economic and social disruptions.

More frequent and severe droughts: Climate change is also causing more frequent and severe droughts in many regions of the world. This can lead to food insecurity, as crops fail and water resources become scarce.

The World's Ability to Adapt to Climate Change

The IPCC's assessment warns that the world is already approaching the limit to which it is able to adapt to severe changes, as weather extremes are "increasingly driving displacement." As climate change continues, the world will face more severe and irreversible consequences. The report emphasizes that immediate action is necessary to avoid reaching the tipping point beyond which the world will no longer be able to adapt to climate change.

The ability of the world to adapt to climate change is limited by several factors. One of the major factors is the lack of resources available to vulnerable populations. Many communities lack the resources to adapt to the impacts of climate change, such as rising sea levels and more frequent and severe droughts. This can lead to displacement and food insecurity.

Another factor that limits the world's ability to adapt to climate change is the lack of political will to address the issue. Climate change is a complex and challenging issue that requires the cooperation of governments, businesses, and individuals. Without strong political leadership, it will be difficult to make the changes necessary to address the climate crisis.

The IPCC's assessment on climate change provides a comprehensive review of the latest scientific research on climate change. The assessment highlights the urgency and severity of the climate crisis, and the need for immediate action to prevent catastrophic consequences. The assessment also provides recommendations for addressing the climate crisis, including a shift towards a low-carbon economy and the adoption of sustainable practices in all sectors of the economy. The impacts of climate change on the environment and society are widespread and severe, and the world's ability to adapt to climate change is limited. Immediate action is necessary to avoid reaching the tipping point beyond which the world will no longer be able to adapt to climate change.

3

The Urgency of Climate Action

The IPCC's Final Warning is a call to action for the entire world to address the climate crisis. The report emphasizes the need for immediate action to prevent catastrophic consequences. This chapter will examine the urgency of climate action, the consequences of inaction, the IPCC's call for a radical transformation of society, and the role of governments, businesses, and individuals in addressing the crisis.

The Need for Immediate Action

The IPCC's assessment is clear: immediate action is needed to prevent catastrophic consequences. Delaying action will result in irreversible consequences that will affect future generations. The need for immediate action is urgent, as the world is already approaching the limit to which it is able to adapt to severe changes.

The consequences of delaying action are severe. Rising temperatures, sea level rise, and extreme weather conditions will lead to the destruction of ecosystems and the displacement of millions of people. The IPCC's assessment warns that the world is already approaching the limit to which it is able to adapt to severe changes, and immediate action is necessary to avoid reaching the tipping point beyond which the world will no longer be able to adapt to climate change.

Consequences of Inaction

The consequences of inaction are severe and far-reaching. The IPCC's assessment warns that delaying action will result in irreversible consequences that will affect future generations. Some of the specific consequences of inaction include:

Rising sea levels: As temperatures rise, glaciers and ice caps are melting, causing sea levels to rise. This can lead to flooding in coastal areas, which can damage infrastructure and homes.

Extreme weather conditions: Climate change is causing more frequent and intense heatwaves, heavy rainfall, and more frequent and severe droughts. These extremes are having a devastating impact on people and the environment, leading to the destruction of homes and livelihoods.

Destruction of ecosystems: Climate change is causing the destruction of ecosystems, including coral reefs, forests, and wetlands. This can lead to the loss of biodiversity and the disruption of ecosystems, which can have severe consequences for human society.

Food insecurity: Climate change is affecting agriculture and food production, leading to food insecurity in many parts of the world. This can lead to malnutrition and starvation, particularly in developing countries.

Health impacts: Climate change is causing an increase in diseases, such as malaria and dengue fever, and is affecting mental health.

The IPCC's Call for a Radical Transformation of Society

To address the climate crisis, the IPCC calls for a radical transformation of society. This transformation requires a shift towards a low-carbon economy, the use of renewable energy sources, and the adoption of sustainable practices in all sectors of the economy.

The IPCC's call for a radical transformation of society is based on the urgency of the climate crisis. Immediate action is necessary to prevent catastrophic consequences. The transformation will require changes in policies, practices, and behaviors at all levels of society.

The Role of Governments, Businesses, and Individuals in Addressing the Crisis

Governments, businesses, and individuals all have a crucial role to play in addressing the climate crisis. Governments must take decisive action to reduce greenhouse gas emissions and promote sustainable practices. Businesses must adopt sustainable practices and invest in renewable energy sources. Individuals can reduce their carbon footprint by adopting sustainable lifestyles and supporting sustainable practices.

Governments have a critical role in addressing the climate crisis. They must implement policies and regulations that reduce greenhouse gas emissions and promote sustainable practices. Governments can also provide funding and support for renewable energy sources and other sustainable practices.

Businesses also have a critical role in addressing the climate crisis. They must adopt sustainable practices and invest in renewable energy sources. Businesses can also provide funding and support for the research and development of new sustainable technologies.

Individuals can also make a difference in addressing the climate crisis. They can reduce their carbon footprint by adopting sustainable lifestyles, such as using public transportation, reducing energy consumption, and supporting sustainable practices. Individuals can also advocate for policy changes and support businesses that prioritize sustainability.

The IPCC's Final Warning emphasizes the urgency and severity of the climate crisis. Immediate action is necessary to prevent catastrophic consequences, and a radical transformation of society is needed to address the crisis. Governments, businesses, and individuals all have a crucial role to play in addressing the climate crisis, and it is important for all of us to take action to prevent irreversible consequences for future generations.

4

Challenges and Barriers to Climate Action

The urgency of the climate crisis requires immediate action to reduce greenhouse gas emissions and prevent catastrophic consequences. However, there are many challenges and barriers to climate action. This chapter will explore the political and economic barriers to climate action, the influence of the fossil fuel industry, technological and infrastructural challenges, and social and psychological barriers to climate action.

Political and Economic Barriers to Climate Action

One of the main barriers to climate action is political and economic. Some governments and businesses are reluctant to take action on climate change because they are concerned about the economic cost of reducing greenhouse gas emissions. Others are resistant to change because of political ideologies or because they do not see climate change as a priority.

Governments and businesses that are resistant to climate action may also be influenced by special interest groups that are opposed to policies that would reduce greenhouse gas emissions. These groups may have a vested interest in maintaining the status quo and may use their political and economic power to block policies that would reduce greenhouse gas emissions.

The Influence of the Fossil Fuel Industry

The fossil fuel industry is one of the main contributors to greenhouse gas emissions. As a result, the industry has a vested interest in maintaining the status quo and resisting policies that would reduce greenhouse gas emissions.

The fossil fuel industry has a significant amount of political and economic power and has used this power to influence public opinion and policy decisions. The industry has funded campaigns and lobbied policymakers to resist policies that would reduce greenhouse gas emissions. The industry has also funded research that casts doubt on the science of climate change.

Technological and Infrastructural Challenges

Another barrier to climate action is technological and infrastructural challenges. Transitioning to a low-carbon economy requires significant investment in renewable energy sources and sustainable infrastructure. However, this transition can be costly and requires significant planning and coordination.

Technological challenges also exist. For example, while renewable energy sources such as wind and solar power are becoming more efficient and cost-effective, they still face technological limitations such as storage and transmission issues.

Overcoming Social and Psychological Barriers

Social and psychological barriers can also hinder climate action. People may resist changing their behaviors and lifestyles because of cultural or social norms. For example, people may resist using public transportation or cycling because they perceive these modes of transportation as inconvenient or uncomfortable.

People may also resist taking action on climate change because of psychological factors such as denial or indifference. Some people may deny the existence of climate change or downplay its severity. Others may feel overwhelmed by the magnitude of the problem and believe that individual actions will not make a difference.

To overcome social and psychological barriers, it is important to communicate the urgency and severity of the climate crisis and to emphasize the role that individuals can play in addressing the problem. Education and awareness campaigns can help to shift social norms and encourage more sustainable behaviors.

The urgency of the climate crisis requires immediate action to reduce greenhouse gas emissions and prevent catastrophic consequences. However, there are many challenges and barriers to climate action, including political and economic barriers, the influence of the fossil fuel industry, technological and infrastructural challenges, and social and psychological barriers. Overcoming these barriers will require a concerted effort from governments, businesses, and individuals to transition to a low-carbon economy and to adopt sustainable practices.

5

Moving Forward

The IPCC's Final Warning highlights the urgent need for immediate action to address the climate crisis. However, the challenges and barriers to climate action can be daunting. This chapter will explore pathways to climate action, successful examples of climate action, addressing climate change as a global issue, and hope for the future.

Pathways to Climate Action

Pathways to climate action require a concerted effort from governments, businesses, and individuals. One pathway is to shift towards a low-carbon economy, which involves transitioning away from fossil fuels and towards renewable energy sources. This transition can be supported by policies and regulations that encourage the use of renewable energy sources and the adoption of sustainable practices.

Another pathway to climate action is to address the root causes of climate change, such as deforestation and industrial agriculture. Addressing these root causes can involve promoting sustainable land use practices and reducing food waste.

Successful Examples of Climate Action

There are many successful examples of climate action that can serve as models for addressing the climate crisis. Some countries have adopted ambitious renewable energy targets and have made significant progress towards transitioning to a low-carbon economy. For example, Iceland is almost entirely powered by renewable energy sources, including geothermal and hydroelectric power.

Cities and municipalities have also taken action to address the climate crisis. Some cities have implemented public transportation systems and bike-sharing programs to reduce carbon emissions from transportation. Other cities have implemented green building standards and policies to reduce energy use in buildings.

Addressing Climate Change as a Global Issue

Addressing the climate crisis requires a global effort. Climate change is a global issue that affects every country and every sector of society. Global cooperation and collaboration are necessary to reduce greenhouse gas emissions and mitigate the impacts of climate change.

International agreements such as the Paris Agreement are important steps towards addressing the climate crisis. The Paris Agreement is a legally binding agreement signed by 195 countries that sets a goal of limiting global warming to well below 2 degrees Celsius above pre-industrial levels, with a target of 1.5 degrees Celsius. The Paris Agreement also includes commitments from countries to reduce greenhouse gas emissions and support climate adaptation measures.

Hope for the Future

Despite the challenges and barriers to climate action, there is hope for the future. Many countries, businesses, and individuals are taking action to reduce greenhouse gas emissions and mitigate the impacts of climate change. Advances in renewable energy technologies are making it increasingly cost-effective to transition to a low-carbon economy.

In addition, there is growing public awareness and concern about the climate crisis. Education and awareness campaigns are helping to shift social norms and encourage more sustainable behaviors. Young people in particular are increasingly engaged in climate activism, pushing for more ambitious action on climate change.

Conclusion

The IPCC's Final Warning is a clarion call to action for the entire world to address the climate crisis. The challenges and barriers to climate action can be daunting, but there are pathways to climate action and successful examples of climate action that can serve as models for addressing the crisis. Addressing the climate crisis requires a global effort and cooperation from governments, businesses, and individuals. Despite the challenges, there is hope for the future, and with concerted effort, the world can transition to a sustainable, low-carbon future.

6

Final Words

The IPCC's Final Warning is a comprehensive assessment of the climate crisis and the urgent need for immediate action. This chapter will provide a recap of the key points covered in this book, final thoughts on the IPCC's Final Warning, and a call to action for governments, businesses, and individuals to address the climate crisis.

Recap of Key Points

The IPCC's Final Warning highlights the urgent need for immediate action to address the climate crisis. The report warns that the world is already approaching the limit to which it is able to adapt to severe changes, and immediate action is necessary to avoid reaching the tipping point beyond which the world will no longer be able to adapt to climate change.

The consequences of delaying action are severe and far-reaching, including rising sea levels, extreme weather conditions, destruction of ecosystems, food insecurity, and health impacts. Addressing the climate crisis requires a global effort and cooperation from governments, businesses, and individuals.

Pathways to climate action include shifting towards a low-carbon economy, addressing the root causes of climate change, and promoting sustainable practices. Successful examples of climate action include countries that have adopted ambitious renewable energy targets and cities that have implemented public transportation systems and green building standards.

Final Thoughts on the IPCC's Final Warning

The IPCC's Final Warning is a wake-up call for the entire world to address the climate crisis. The report highlights the urgency of the crisis and the severe consequences of delaying action. The report also emphasizes the need for a radical transformation of society and a global effort to reduce greenhouse gas emissions and mitigate the impacts of climate change.

While the challenges and barriers to climate action can be daunting, there are pathways to climate action and successful examples of climate action that can serve as models for addressing the crisis. Advances in renewable energy technologies and growing public awareness and concern about the climate crisis provide hope for the future.

Call to Action

The IPCC's Final Warning is a call to action for governments, businesses, and individuals to address the climate crisis. Governments must take decisive action to reduce greenhouse gas emissions and promote sustainable practices. Businesses must adopt sustainable practices and invest in renewable energy sources. Individuals can reduce their carbon footprint by adopting sustainable lifestyles and supporting sustainable practices.

The urgency of the climate crisis requires immediate action. Delaying action will result in irreversible consequences that will affect future generations. It is the responsibility of all of us to take action to address the climate crisis and transition to a sustainable, low-carbon future.

The IPCC's Final Warning is a clarion call to action for the entire world to address the climate crisis. The report highlights the urgency of the crisis, the consequences of delaying action, and the need for a radical transformation of society. While the challenges and barriers to climate action can be daunting, there are pathways to climate action and successful examples of climate action that provide hope for the future. The time for action is now, and it is the responsibility of all of us to take action to address the climate crisis.

7

Glossary

Climate Change - Refers to a long-term shift in global or regional weather patterns, specifically to changes in temperature, precipitation, and other weather conditions that occur over several decades or longer.

Greenhouse Gases - Gases that trap heat in the Earth's atmosphere and contribute to the greenhouse effect. The most common greenhouse gases are carbon dioxide, methane, and nitrous oxide.

IPCC - The Intergovernmental Panel on Climate Change is a scientific body established by the United Nations to assess climate change.

Renewable Energy - Energy that comes from sources that are replenished naturally, such as wind, solar, and geothermal energy.

Low-Carbon Economy - An economy that produces low levels of greenhouse gas emissions.

Paris Agreement – An international agreement signed in 2015 by 195 countries that sets a goal of limiting global warming to well below 2 degrees Celsius above pre-industrial levels, with a target of 1.5 degrees Celsius.

Mitigation – Actions taken to reduce greenhouse gas emissions and slow the pace of climate change.

Adaptation – Actions taken to reduce the impacts of climate change on human societies and ecosystems.

Climate Resilience – The ability of human societies and ecosystems to adapt to changing climate conditions and withstand the impacts of climate change.

Carbon Budget – The maximum amount of carbon dioxide that can be emitted into the atmosphere while still remaining within a certain temperature threshold.

About the Author

Avery Wright is an enigmatic figure who is an author in the fields of AI, Technology, and the Arts. A combat veteran of the US Army, Avery has almost two decades of experience in the IT industry, which has given them a unique perspective on the intersection of technology and society.

As an author, Avery has published a range of books on topics such as the future of AI, the role of drones in modern warfare, and the medicinal properties of mushrooms. Their writing often explores the cutting-edge of technology and how it is changing the world around us. Avery's work is notable for its depth and insight, as well as its ability to make complex topics accessible to a broad audience.

Away from the world of writing, Avery is a private individual who values their privacy. Despite this, they remain a voice in the tech industry and beyond. Whether sharing their thoughts on the latest developments in AI or commenting on the state of the world, Avery's perspective is always worth listening to.

You can connect with me on:

🌐 https://sirexodia.wixsite.com/avery-wright
🐦 https://twitter.com/AveryWrightAI
📘 https://www.facebook.com/profile.php?id=100089987171726
🔗 https://www.amazon.com/author/averywrightai

Subscribe to my newsletter:

✉ https://sirexodia.wixsite.com/avery-wright

Also by Avery Wright

Also by Avery Wright
  "Mastering Midjourney AI: The Beginner's Handbook"
  "Chat GPT: A Digital Journey Begins"
  "AI and the Art of Binary"
  "Mycological Marvels: Exploring the Art of AI-Created Mushrooms"
  "AI in Healthcare: How Artificial Intelligence is Transforming Medicine"
  "Transformative Art:: A Journey with Artificial Intelligence"
  "From Predator to Phantom: A Glimpse At Drones"
  "AI and the Future of Humanity"
  "The Tao of Inner Peace"
  "Taoism Unleashed: Advanced Concepts for Deepening Your Practice"
  "The Knife's Edge:: A View on the Ultra Rich and their Motivations"
  "Defending the Skies: The Rise of Unidentified Aerial Phenomena and the Battle for Airspace Dominance"
  "Mastering the Board: The Power of Pawns in Chess"
  "The Brain in the Machine: Understanding the Inner Workings of Artificial Intelligence"
  "Healing with Fungi: The Science of Medicinal Mushrooms"
  "Chat GPT: ChatGPT Explores the World: Conversations Across Cultures"
  "Chat GPT: Unleashing ChatGPT's Power: Navigating the Digital Realm"

Avery Wright's work spans a range of topics, from the cutting-

edge of AI and technology to the ancient practice of Taoism
and the art of chess. Their books are notable for their depth,
insight, and ability to make complex topics accessible to a broad
audience. With almost two decades of experience in the IT field
and a background as a combat veteran, Avery brings a unique
perspective to their writing that is both informative and thought-
provoking. Whether you are interested in exploring the frontiers
of technology or deepening your understanding of the human
experience, Avery's books are a must-read.

**Mastering Midjourney AI - The Beginner's
Handbook**
Mastering Midjourney AI: The Beginner's
Handbook is a comprehensive guide for
beginners looking to learn about the Midjourney AI platform and how to use it
for image generation. The book covers a
range of topics, including understanding
Midjourney AI's parameters and settings, using URLs for image
inspiration, adjusting image quality, and more.
https://www.amazon.com/dp/B0BV8PGDXT

AI in Healthcare: How Artificial Intelligence is Transforming Medicine

Discover the groundbreaking impact of AI in healthcare. From personalized medicine to revolutionizing the healthcare workforce, AI is changing the game. Get a deeper understanding of its current and future applications and the ethical, legal, and social implications in "AI in Healthcare: How Artificial Intelligence is Transforming Medicine." Get your copy now on Amazon!
https://www.amazon.com/dp/B0BTBZDVBY

Mycological Marvels: Exploring the Art of AI-Created Mushrooms

Mycological Marvels: Exploring the Art of AI-Created Mushrooms" showcases stunning AI-generated mushroom art and delves into the technical & creative aspects of this innovative form of art. A celebration of beauty & technology in the world of art.
https://www.amazon.com/dp/B0BVFS2MNX

Transformative Art - A Journey with Artificial Intelligence

Transformative Art: A Journey with AI is a visually stunning and thought-provoking book that explores the intersection of artificial intelligence and the world of art. The book features breathtaking images of futuristic cities, technology, vehicles, robots, flying ships, conceptual art, abstract art, and unique pieces, all within the context of transformative art. Each chapter begins with a powerful quote that sets the tone for a deep dive into the themes of perception, change, reflection, risk-taking, emotional connection, the journey within, and the universal language of art. The book is written by Avery Wright, a talented author with a passion for exploring the ways in which technology is changing our lives and our world. This book is a must-read for anyone interested in the intersection of art, technology, and the human experience. https://www.amazon.com/dp/B0BTWNYLJD

**Defending the Skies: The Rise of Uniden-
tified Aerial Phenomena and the Battle for
Airspace Dominance**

"Unidentified aerial phenomena, or UAPs,
have been on the rise in recent years, leading
to increased concerns over airspace security
and national defense. This book delves into
the recent incidents of weather balloon take-
downs across North America, the establishment of the UAP Task
Force, and the potential implications for scientific exploration
and national security. With a focus on the search for answers
about UAPs, this book provides a comprehensive overview of
the rise of UAP sightings and their potential impact on human
understanding and society."
https://www.amazon.com/dp/B0BW5JD7WT

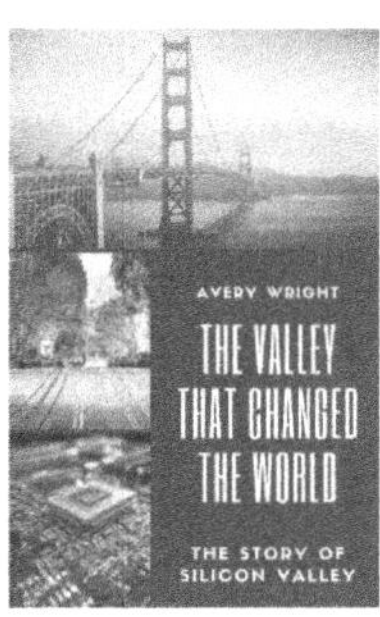

The Valley that Changed the World

"The Valley that Changed the World" is a
comprehensive exploration of the history of
Silicon Valley, from its origins as a center
for agriculture and defense to its emergence
as the global epicenter of the technology
industry. The book delves into the stories of
the pioneers and innovators who helped to
shape the region, including the founders of companies like Intel,
Apple, Google, and Facebook. Through their stories, readers
will gain a deeper understanding of the forces that transformed
Silicon Valley into the world-changing phenomenon it is today.
https://www.amazon.com/dp/B0BYCXY2R6

Mastering Prompt Engineering for Chat-GPT: A Beginner's Guide (ChatGPT Master-class)

Mastering Prompt Engineering for ChatGPT: A Beginner's Guide" is a comprehensive guide to prompt engineering for ChatGPT. Whether you're a beginner or an experienced user, this book will provide you with the principles and best practices to effectively guide ChatGPT towards generating accurate and relevant responses in a variety of use cases. From understanding the capabilities and limitations of ChatGPT to crafting effective prompts and evaluating their effectiveness, this book covers all the essential topics and strategies you need to master prompt engineering for ChatGPT.

https://www.amazon.com/dp/B0BWYTJ8B8

www.ingramcontent.com/pod-product-compliance
Lightning Source LLC
Chambersburg PA
CBHW071029260726
48662CB00024B/2161